REAL IRELAND

"REAL IRELAND"

Photographs • Liam Blake

Text • Brendan Kennelly

Appletree Press

First published in Ireland by the Appletree Press
Ltd, 7 James Street South, Belfast BT2 8DL.
This paperback edition first published in 1988
by The Appletree Press Ltd. Printed in Italy.
Photographs ©Liam Blake 1984.
Text © Brenden Kennelly 1984.
All rights reserved.

British Library Cataloguing in Publication Data
Blake, Liam, *1952-*
Real Ireland.
1. Ireland. Social life
I. Title II. Kennelly, Brendan, *1936-*
941. 50824

ISBN 0-86281-205-4

9 8 7 6 5 4 3 2 1

CONTENTS

DUBLIN

'THERE were three people with me: two Irishmen and a Dublinman.' Thus, Brendan Behan making a point in a debate with fellow-playwright John B. Keane, to raise runds for an Orphanage, one October evening in 1959, in the Ballroom of the Shelbourne Hotel in Dublin. With these words, Behan, the witty, boisterous, great-hearted Dubliner, expressed a cultural partition almost as profound and far-reaching in its implications as the political partition that splits the island. Even the structure of this book with its sharp, lyrical photographs bears out what I say. It's Dublin first and the Rest after. Dublin versus the Rest. The men on the Hill versus the men from the mountains. Fish and chips against bacon and cabbage. Jackeen against culchie. And why not? Isn't rivalry the seed of friendship? Is there any Dub as passionate as the converted culchie? Is there any culchie as deep-rooted as the converted Dub? (To be honest, however, there are relatively few of the latter, although you'll find examples of that rare, vehement breed scattered from Dingle to Donegal.)

But why? What is the source of the Dub's need to assert his identity with such eloquent insistence, such defiance and bravado, against the world? 'Beyond the Red Cow Inn, they eat their young.' Behan again. Needless to say, at *this* side of the Red Cow Inn, the young are looked after with scrupulous care, despite the occasional glue-sniffing orgy. Out there is the wild, child-scoffing jungle. In here is Dublin, our fair city, our Liffey-purged lady, our great, patched, warm overcoat that we wear with pride and affection, our mother scarred but surviving, our Capital of crack, our stage where we all act our parts with gusto and individuality, our arena where verbal gladiators dazzle and dance. But why does the Dub constantly harp on his uniqueness? My own view is that, at some level, that most engaging of articulate animals feels threatened by the alien rustic hordes that surround him. He is a king menaced by subjects who constantly threaten to surpass and overthrow him. Here he is, in his very own city, menaced by ambitious legions. Dublin is a magnet. The irony is that this magnetic power poses a threat to the Dubliner's cherished sense of uniqueness. The hypnotic drawing power of his city is, paradoxically, the truest source of his insecurity. It may well be that for the Dubliner, Dublin is an ambiguous mother.

And yet there is no doubting the Dubliner's 'born and bred' loyalty to that same ambiguous mum. *Ulysses* is an expression of that loyalty in universally imaginative terms. There have been many great poets of urban life. One thinks of Blake writing of the 'mind-forged manacles' evident in the faces of people in nineteenth-century industrial London; of Baudelaire contemplating the seething anonymity of the Paris crowds; of Eliot staring at the multitudes pouring purposefully, or purposelessly, over London Bridge; of Hart Crane at once lost and inspired in the mad miracle of New York. But surely, of all writers that have written of cities, James Joyce is the most comprehensive, penetrating and enduring. It is nothing short of a heroic achievement. And no small reason for that achievement is Joyce's characteristic obsession with Dublin, *as a Dubliner,* and not merely as a great experimental novelist. Joyce is the ultimate Dubliner, convinced that Dublin 'is the centre of the paralysis of the universe'. There's a marvellous, black egotism in that conviction. Whatever about the paralysis (and I for one would argue that *Ulysses* is more about abundant life than about any form of death) there is no doubting the fact that Joyce looked upon Dublin as the centre of his own imaginative universe, and in so doing, placed his native city at the centre of twentieth century literature. Despite his immense learning and knowledge, despite his genius for language and languages, Joyce is, in one sense, the most articulate representative of that noble body of Dubliners who still assert that 'Beyond the Red Cow Inn they eat their young', and who also make the innocent-eyed suggestion to occupying culchies, 'Why don't yez all scarper off home and snag a few turnips!'

It may well be that Joyce's obsession with Dublin demanded that he leave it. Would familiarity have killed his interest and his plans? Did he sense some danger there,

some threat to his literary ambition? Did he actually feel that he too might be paralysed imaginatively if he remained physically in or near the 'centre of the paralysis of the universe'? Whatever it was, he got out and stayed out. It could be argued that Joyce went into exile to escape his own destruction as a writer. Anyone who knows Dublin knows there is a really vicious, destructive side to the city. For Yeats, it was a city where a life's reputation could be lost 'between the night and morning', a city 'where motley is worn' and slanderous gossip is chewed as though it were the best of Bewley's brown bread. For Brendan Behan, it was a city that filled a man with loneliness but deprived him of solitude. For Patrick Kavanagh, it was 'malignant Dublin' that introduced him to the dull, humiliating grind of poverty and forced him to borrow a shilling from a neighbour, pretending the money was for the gas when in fact it went to buy a chop for the hungry poet. Recently, an Irish writer living in London said that if he remained in Dublin he'd be an alcoholic within six months. Writers have an eye for beauty; they also have a nose for danger. And Dublin *is* dangerous. The problem is to recognize that fact; the solution is up to the individual. My own view is that without this danger Dublin would not be Dublin. Where there is danger there is a need to dare. And daring is the hall-mark of a living imagination. There is no running away any more. Writers must face that complex Dublin music and make their own music out of it. The time for running and blaming is past. The time for staying and creating is now.

As real and indisputable as Dublin's destructive tendencies are its many creative abilities and opportunities. The centre of the paralysis of the universe contains deep and genuine creative energies. These energies are everywhere, if only we have the patience and alertness to seek them out, encourage and develop them. First and foremost, they are in ourselves. A lot of young artists (I am using that term in its broadest sense) have discovered and are discovering that marvellous and normal reality. Youngsters, using chalks of different colours, copy masterpieces on to pavements. ('Hope the bleedin' rain keeps off!') Chaplinesque figures create their own open-air theatre in Grafton Street, competing with singers and players and clowns and other actors. A poet plans a broadsheet (as he tentatively asks a likely victim for the loan of another fiver!). In a time of depression and inflation, there is talk of new plays. A novelist swears he'll be out of this hell-hole and living in London or Paris within four days. Four weeks and two chapters later, he is still making the same resolution. Here is a play from a girl serving a long sentence in Limerick Prison. Here is a sheaf of poems from a young man in Mountjoy Jail. And here, from London, are five short stories from a bristling young Dubliner who is fed-up to the teeth with all 'those bloody Irish short stories' and who is determined, like some latter-day Ezra Pound, to 'make 'em new'. As always, such activity is accompanied by dreary cynicism and equally dreary sentimentality, by lethargy, depression and despair. Dublin has an apparently endless supply of sedentary cynics whose sole function in life appears to be to make some destructive comment on every creative effort. The creative impulse is a good swimmer in a treacherous sea. Nobody would deny Dublin its fair or unfair quota of treachery; but it would be foolish to deny that there are quite a few good swimmers knocking about as well. Sink or swim. There is, as always, a choice. Or there appears to be.

There is one area in which Dubliners do not have, and do not wish to have a choice, and that is in the matter of language. When it comes to words, most Dubliners are addicts and their addiction is lifelong. Quite simply, they are in love with words or, more precisely, with the sounds of words. They do not object to meaning; but their joyous use of language is never inhibited or limited if the meaning happens to be distorted or even lost. To my mind and ear, this cavalier attitude to meaning pays marvellous linguistic dividends. It clears the way for these happy verbal accidents that make poetry possible in ordinary conversation. This is really a question of feeling free in the presence of language. Language can be an inhibiting, even a crippling force; (it is such a fear that gives rise to Schools of Elocution); but language can also be an exultant, liberating power. Great Dublin writers such as Mangan, Shaw, O'Casey, Joyce and Flann O'Brien recognize and exploit this fact. Shaw's book *On Language*, with its mixture of didactic passion towards, and comic detachment from language and its uses could never have been written by an Englishman because no Englishman knows or experiences the language in the way that Shaw does. Shaw wanted to rewrite and revitalize the English language, and in stating his case, allows both his love of language and his criticism of its uses and abuses to emerge with typical impish energy.

> When we begin by refusing to spell as we pronounce we end by having to pronounce as we spell. The etymologists, to show the French origin of the word oblige, refused to spell it phonetically; and a generation of superior persons despise those who did not say obleege, and were themselves despised by a still more select circle who said obleezh. But who dares say obleege now, except Joseph Surface on the stage? The history of the word envelope tells the same story. Ongvelope and Ann Velope have had their day; we spelt it ennvelope and now we have to pronounce it ennvelope. The American reformers want us to spell

catalogue catalog, a word in such common use that its pronunciation has been traditionally maintained in spite of the spelling. But what of epilog and prolog? These two words, which most Englishmen never utter or hear uttered in their lives, and the rest use perhaps once in 20 years, are on those rare occasions mispronounced, nine times out of ten, as epiloag and proloag. As the working classes become literate and please themselves by dragging into ordinary conversation more and more long words which they have never heard pronounced, they introduce ways of their own of pronouncing them, founded necessarily on the spelling. Programme, a vulgarism which offends the eye as Paris pronounced Paree in English offends the ear, has been in my hearing pronounced so as to rhyme to Damn me. That is how we shall all have to pronounce it some day. I foresee the time when I shall be forced to pronounce semi-conscious as See my Conscious. Then there is the march of preciosity. Already I blush when habit betrays me into calling clothes cloze. I have heard a tenor pronouncing the I in Handel's Where e'er you walk. If Detford has become Depped Ford in spite of usage, I see no reason to doubt that det will presently become debbed. I am fond of the word ham, meaning a country place larger than a hamlet. I am still allowed to speak of East Ham and West Ham, because the words are written separately; but when I speak of Lewis Ham, Elt Ham, or Peters Ham, I am suspected of a defect in my speech, almost as if I had spoken of Cars Halton (properly rhyming to Walton) instead of Ker Shalltn. The received pronunciations nowadays are Louis Sham, Peter Sham, L. Tham, and so on. And the people who support the bad spelling which is corrupting the language in this fashion pretend to have a special regard for it, and prattle of the Bible and Shakespeare! They remind me of a New York Police commissioner who once arrested a whole theatrical company for performing one of my plays, and explained, on being remonstrated with, that the Sermon on the Mount was good enough for him.

Joyce went further. In *Finnegans Wake*, he actually created a language, rich, musical, miraculously playful, devastatingly funny and truly lyrical. Joyce brought language so close to music that the best way to read *Finnegans Wake* is probably the Dubliner's own twinkling, hypothetical way: 'You could sing that one if you had an air to it'. In *Finnegans Wake*, sound is all; and because Joyce is true to sound and sounds, meaning and meanings flow through his book without laying their heavy philosophical paws on his poetry. Far from being a 'heavy' book, *Finnegans Wake* is a beautiful lightsome thing, an epic song, the soul music of a Dublin Homer giving full vent to his deepest and most obsessive love, the love of words.

Do writers, born in specific places, concentrate and give fuller, deeper expression to prevailing popular attitudes to, and uses of language, in the complex and difficult process of creating their own literary language? I believe they do. Joyce's famous formula for the conditions of lasting artistic creation, 'Silence, exile and cunning' is not quite accurate or complete, though endlessly mentioned. Joyce was not an especially cunning man; but he was a very punning one. 'Silence, exile and punning' is closer to the Joycean actuality. Punning is as deep and real a part of Dublin life as the sniffy Liffey. With you in a jiffey. There are those who hold that punning is the lowest form of wit; but to the word-loving Dubliner punning is a way of life. He cherishes it, revels in it, mocks and infuriates with it, tantalizes and amuses with it, praises and damns with it. For the trueblue Dub, punning is playing, a mental mischief, pure verbal fun, a linguistic dance based on the enlightening possibilities of word-distortion, word-manipulation. So rejoice becomes read Joyce, Ulysses itself becomes useless, and you never say a cross word about a Crossword. Nobody would love this distorting playfulness more than the punning exile himself. An inevitable consequence of all this is the Dubliner's love of anecdotes, 'yarns', little chuckling, gossipy stories. When a Dubliner says 'Did ya hear this one?' he is not asking a question, he is inviting himself to tell you his latest yarn. Being button-holed by such a man can be a pleasant enough experience; it can also be a boring one. But there is no way out. A Dubliner with a yarn is a man with a mission, impossible to stop, so you might as well submit and listen. There's always the possibility that it might be 'good for a laugh'. That little phrase captures something about life in Dublin which can sometimes be heartening and sometimes sinister, especially at those moments when everything, even forms of human suffering, are 'good for a laugh'. One's own suffering may well be, especially in retrospect; I'm not so sure about the sufferings of others.

Something no Dubliner suffers from, when it comes to making claims for his ability with language, is modesty. 'Oi undertand,' says he, 'that the most perfect English in the world is spoken in Dublin. Dalkey, to be precise.' I have heard similar claims made for Killiney, Foxrock, Stillorgan, Blackrock and Ballsbridge (or Pons Testiculorum as classical Dubliners Latinize that lofty spot). This is a harmless myth. My own experience, however, says that some of 'the best English' can be heard in Inchicore, Bluebell, Stoneybatter, Suffolk Street and the Coombe. After all, it may well be that 'the best English' is the English that gives you 'a bit of a laugh'.

Laughter is a prominent part of Dublin life, though I have heard foreign friends say that Dubliners, especially in winter, show gloomy, doomy faces to the world. Perhaps. All the same, anyone who takes the time to observe the faces in the streets of Dublin will observe many faces that are accustomed to smiling. (One criticism I would make of the Dublin section of this book is that there are not enough faces in it.) I know certain faces that come startingly and genuinely alive with humour, and this is a gift to brighten even the rainiest, dirtiest Dublin day. And there are days in Dublin which one can only call, without the slightest reservation, absolutely dirty. Such days are achievements in filth. Buildings turn deathly grey, streets become relentlessly dreary, rain falls and falls and falls, the filth-thickened air becomes difficult to swallow, so it's no wonder that hot whiskey and cool Guinness become the solace of thousands. But then, thanks to the unpredictability of our weather, the next day will probably have soft sunshine and there may well be a glamorous story-book quality transfiguring yesterday's squalor. Just as there are incredibly dirty days in Dublin, so also can there be days of purest delight. Perhaps these are the days on which one notices the laughter.

What often strikes me on such days, particularly at evening, is the quality of the light in the streets. If I were a painter I would never cease to paint that light as it plays in the streets, on the houses, in the rivers and the canals. It seems, almost, to be a light of revelation; and it is truly mesmeric.

There are moments when the light
Makes me start up, fright
In my heart as if I feared to see
Unbearable clarity about me.
Once, on Portobello Bridge,
I had the sudden privilege
Of seeing light leap from the sky
About five o'clock on an autumn day,
Defining every visible thing,
Unseen by one among the moving throng;
Road, bridge, factory, canal,

Stained swans and filthy reeds, all
The set homegoing faces
Filling motorcars and buses;
Then I knew that energy is but
Unconsciousness; if moving man could
See where they are going, they would
Stop and contemplate the light
And never move again until
They understood why it should spill
A sudden benediction on
The head of every homegoing man.
But no-one looked or saw the way
The waters danced for the visiting light
Or how green foliage glittered. It
Was ignored completely.
I knew the world is most at ease
With acceptable insanities,
Important nothings that command
The heart and mind of busy men
Who, had they seen it, might have praised
the light on Portobello Bridge.
But then, light broke. I looked. An evening glow.
Men go home because they do not know.

As one grows to know and love this old city, one must admit that one's fondness for its character is inseparable from one's appreciation of its inhabitants. Dublin combines the intimacy of a village with the advantages, risks and anonymity of a metropolis. Therefore, it draws strong and frequently polar responses. 'A great city to get out of' says one man, while another swears that he 'wouldn't be caught dead anywhere else'! But it is precisely these opposed responses, these daily little conflicts in loyalty, that help to account for the fascination that Dublin holds for many people. 'They always come back' smiles an old Dubliner, referring to returning visitors. Not all come back, but quite a few do. Dublin has its own undeniable magnetism.

To-day, Dublin retains that magnetic character while looking more and more outwards to Europe. The years ahead are bound to see many changes in the life and culture of the city but it is to be hoped that the relaxed humanity, humour, conversation and sheer decency of so many of its citizens will survive all changes, no matter how subtle or sophisticated, and deepen steadily with the years.

One of the wrought iron lampstands on
Grattan Bridge.

Smithfield Market.

Schoolhouse Lane West, off High Street.

Bewley's Cafe, Westmoreland Street.

Mulligan's Pub, Poolbeg Street.

Bridges over the river Liffey.

Moore Street vegetable market.

Reflections of the Bank of Ireland headquarters, Baggot Street.

A section of the Bord na Mona office block, Baggot Street.

Itinerants in Bride Street.

Hubband Bridge in winter,
over the Grand Canal.

Hoardings on St. Stephen's Green.

Hoardings on St. Stephen's Green.

Graffiti in the Francis Street area.

Roof top clothes line at Kelly's Corner.

The Dub's after the football final, Drumcondra.

Shrine in O'Connell Street.

City skyline from Grattan Bridge.

Clery's Bar, Amiens Street.

The Four Courts, Inns Quay.

Custom House reflected in the river Liffey.

The People's Garden, Phoenix Park.

Georgian house, St. Stephen's Green.

Shop front, Wexford Street.

In Smith's Bar, Dun Laoghaire, Co. Dublin.

Trinity College.

Christ Church Cathedral at dusk.

Howth Pier, Co. Dublin.

Sandymount Strand, Dublin Bay.

TOWN & COUNTRY

THE end of this golden summer of 1983 ('Tis like a good dream' an old woman said to me) is as apt a time as any to reflect on the fact that the Irish countryside, with its towns and villages, is undergoing a number of changes that have already left their mark on a notoriously traditional and conservative way of life. Rural Irish conservatism is of a special kind and can be understood, if at all, only through deep and constant study of Irish history. We have heard plenty about 'the centuries of oppression' to which the native Irish were subjected. I would like to say straightaway that my admiration for the people of the Irish countryside is the special admiration one reserves for gifted survivors such as Jews, Blacks or women all over the globe. A quick glimpse at some of the main events of the past four centuries will illustrate what I mean. In the seventeenth century the Cromwellian campaign against the native Irish was a campaign of disciplined and merciless savagery, a campaign which ensured that the name of Cromwell would forever be the most hated name on the lips of Irish people. The Penal Laws of the eighteenth century were a systematic attempt to annihilate the legal identity of Irish Catholics;

it is no exaggeration to say that these laws against Irish Catholics resemble Hitler's approach to the extermination of Jews. The nineteenth century brought the Great Famine; in fact, it brought several famines. During that century, the population of Ireland was almost halved. In this century, Ireland experienced, among other traumas, Revolution and Civil War. The Irish people survived all these catastrophes. They are to be admired for that. But what are the consequences on the Irish character of these and many other catastrophes? God alone knows. Confronted with such accumulated tragedy, a man can only say what he thinks and sees. That is what I propose to do.

A people who have been long dispossessed of their land and who, after many battles, succeed in retrieving it, will thereafter have an especially passionate attachment to it. It is hard to over-emphasize the importance of land in the Irish countryside. Such are the passions which disputes over land arouse that people have often killed for it. Sometimes, only a relatively small amount of land might be in question but, large or small, the aroused passions burn with undiminished intensity. One of the dramatists who have dealt most incisively with Irish rural life is John

B. Keane; and Keane's most powerful play is *The Field*, a compelling dramatization of these passions I have mentioned. In passing, and by logical extension, *The Field* is also a study of the immense differences between law and justice, and between the laws for the rich and the laws for the poor. Land and law. Anybody who would like to have more than a tourist knowledge of rural Ireland should consider, at some length, these two related matters.

In the Irish countryside everything, while often appearing daft and disconnected on the surface, is intricately and definitely connected to everything else. Take, again, that question of land. The most explosive long poem written in Ireland during the first half of this century, *The Great Hunger*, by Patrick Kavanagh, deals with the connections between land, religion, family and sex. It is basically a poem about the lifelong physical and spiritual castration of a small farmer who is dominated by his mother, slavish to his Church, and whose life is a pathetic round of hard work, furtive masturbation, Sunday morning respectability, and dedication to the land that grows bleak in Winter and blossoms in Spring while the central figure himself, Paddy Maguire, 'a fourteen-hour day', shrivels into a sad parody of a man, a respectable old scarecrow, a 'ragged sculpture of the wind'. Many Irishmen, exactly like Maguire, have given their bodies and souls to land and have never shaped any living human relationships, sexual or otherwise. There is a terrible irony in this. Land is a generous giver but an insatiate taker. It will give food and nurture and even a certain spiritual consolation; but land will take, with a silence old and deep as itself, the best days of a man's life, his blood and sweat, his body's strength and his mind's attention. And it will swallow him silently in the end. Land can exhilarate and thrill; but it can also keep a man trapped in the cage of his unconscious life. Over the years, he can become a prisoner in that cage, a prisoner whose true tragedy is that he has forgotten what freedom is. He can become a willing slave, enchained to what will wear him down as surely as Winter closes every year. There is at least one force that can free Irish farmers from this situation; and that is education. And the welcome truth nowadays is that more and more 'people of the land' are involving themselves in the kind of education that will help them to approach land in a new, more enlightened way. But in dealing with almost any Irish farmer, particulary as you drift Westwards, it is well to remember that behind his eyes are the ghosts of famine, Penal Laws and Land Wars, and that his skilful use of the Béal Bocht, or Poor Mouth, the ever-ready whine of opportunism, the instinctive political exploitation of a poverty old as history – his skilful use of all these things means they are the weapons of the survivor, the man who, though he may have it good just now, once had it very bad indeed. So bad, in fact, that he cannot exclude the possibility that he may have it pretty bad in the future. So, achree, 'tis better to play safe. After all, you'd never know. . .

Playing safe. Caution. Think of the Pension. Look to the rainy day. Take it nice an' aisy, boy. Make no statements. You can never tell. Send your mother a pound. Anyone who has lived in the Irish countryside will be aware of this caution and of the narrow materialism it can lead to. This caution has its comic aspects, especially in the sexual area ('I never got married; the winters were too short'). But it can also be very sad. This caution is connected also with a kind of steadfast mindlessness, a frightening vacancy of mind which leads inevitably to slavish obedience to the authority of Church and State. And yet, it is not as simple as that, because, co-existing with that mental vacancy one can often find a paradoxical healthy scepticism, a startling detachment from *all* authority. If pyschological contradictions can be explained, I suggest that, in Ireland at least, history is a helpful guide.

This sun-blessed summer of 1983 confirmed what I have always known; Ireland is one of the most beautiful little countries in the world. It is, however, a beauty riddled with shadows. Not all of these shadows are sinister, though some are. One shadow which, when you think of it, is much more than a shadow, is the past. To travel through the Irish countryside is not only to see many genial people and a magical landscape; it is also to journey through the past while remaining in the present, a delightful experiment in moving perspective. Every parish in Ireland is rich with the presence of the past and its evidences. Once, going by train from Dublin to Limerick, I saw the past turning its pages over for me on the journey, and I read what I saw, fascinated. Travelling on the Limerick train was a journey through time.

Hurtling between hedges now, I see
Green desolation stretch on either hand
While sunlight blesses all magnanimously.

The gods and heroes are gone for good and
Men evacuate each Munster valley
And midland plain, gravelly Connaught land

And Leinster town. Who, I wonder, fully
Understands the imminent predicament,
Sprung from rooted suffering and folly?

Broken castles tower, lost order's monument,
Splendour crumbling in sun and rain,
Witnesses to all we've squandered and spent.

But no Phoenix rises from that ruin
Although the wild furze in yellow pride
Explodes in bloom above each weed and stone,

Promise ablaze on every mountainside
After the centuries' game of pitch-and-toss

Separates what must live from what has died.

A church whips past, proclaiming heavy loss
Amounting to some forty thousand pounds;
A marble Christ unpaid for on His Cross

Accepts the Limerick train's irreverent sound,
Relinquishes great power to little men –
A river flowing still, but underground.

Wheels clip the quiet counties. Now and then
I see a field where like an effigy
In rushy earth, there stands a man alone

Lifting his hand in salutation. He
Disappears almost as soon as he is seen,
Drowned in distant anonymity.

We have travelled far, the journey has been
Costly, tormented odyssey through night;
And now, noting the unmistakable green,

The pools and trees that spring into the sight,
The sheep that scatter madly, wheel and run,
Quickly transformed to terrified leaping white,

I think of what the land has undergone
And find the luminous events of history
Intolerable as staring at the sun.

Only twenty miles to go and I'll be
Home. Seeing two crows low over the land,
I recognize the land's uncertainty,

The unsensational surrender and
Genuflection to the busy stranger
Whose power in pocket brings him power in hand.

Realizing now how dead is anger
Such as sustained us at the very start
With possibility in time of danger,

I know why we have turned away, apart
(I'm moving still but so much time has sped)
From the dark realities of the heart.

From my window now, I try to look ahead
And know, remembering what's been done and said
That we must always cherish, and reject, the dead.

Some people dwell so much in the past that it becomes a stifling force in their lives. Others turn their backs on it, ignore it, and as a result, have a very distorted view of the present. As I said at the end of that poem, one must try both to cherish *and* reject the past; not to become stifled by disproportionate brooding; not to become uncomprehending through wilful neglect. There are many beautiful photographs in this book which capture the subtle, enduring influence of the past on the lives of people in the Irish countryside to-day. These photographs should not just be looked at; they should be studied.

I mentioned, in writing of Dublin, that it is a city of talk and talkers. Dublin talk tends to be witty and reasonably direct; country talk tends to be humorous and indirect. Where talkers gather, there will usually be drink. And in the Irish countryside, in towns and villages, at weddings, wakes, funerals, at all sporting events and festivals, indeed wherever friends and acquaintances meet, the talk flows and so does the drink. 'When do the pubs close in Ballybunion?' somebody asks a local. 'After the Listowel Races' comes the reply. Where's the respect for law there, will you tell me? In that same Listowel, there's a marvellous annual hosting of scribblers called *Writers' Week*. It could with almost equal accuracy be called *Talkers' Week*. Talking and sipping the night through is one of the most civilized aspects of life in rural Ireland.

During the forties and fifties, Irish writers tended to present life in the countryside as a boring, dull, repressed, gossipy, trivial, mean affair. There was a great deal of truth in that. There still is; and writers must always specify and probe these ills. But nowadays there is often a much more lighthearted note struck in that life. Festivals abound in many towns. And the most important aspect of these festivals is that they involve thousands of young people. Thirty and forty years ago, people emigrated from Ireland in countless thousands; nowadays, they tend to stay at home, not only because other countries no longer offer apparently endless employment but because young Irish people feel more and more that Ireland is *their* country, with all its problems, challenges, deprivations and disadvantages as well as its openings, opportunities and hopes. This is one of the healthiest signs of contemporary Irish life. The spectacle of youth flowing out of the countryside was a truly tragic sight; it was like watching a strong body being drained of its blood. It can only be for the future good of this island that youngsters put their energy back into the land that nurtured them. That is healthy and sane. Besides, it'll get rid of a lot of sentimental songs about exile and sending money home to your mother. Poor mother machree was very fond of the lolly.

The two most powerful forces in rural Ireland today are the Catholic Church and the Gaelic Athletic Association. Though the power of both these institutions has waned somewhat during the past fifteen years, they still dominate rural life to a large extent. As always, the Church is conservative, stolid and unintellectual, though many of the priests, especially the younger ones, are not afraid to show their individuality. But priests are a bit like civil servants and academics; as they get promoted, they become more cautious. There's that word 'caution' again. Where have all these wild romantic Irishmen vanished to? Into suburbia, I fear. And they have become senior executives and professors and parish priests and bishops. And suddenly they are quiet. And cautious. Why is caution so like timidity? Why is it so offensive to the imagination?

Why are Irish priests so lacking in imaginative daring? If they want an attractive church they must use their imaginations, let them rip a little. Most genuinely holy people are very daring, instinctive, revolutionaries. And their most serious revolutions are always conducted against themselves, against their own lethargy, boringness, indifference and drooping spirits. That's why people see them as exemplary.

Catholicism is the religion of something like ninety-six per cent of the population but the next religion isn't far behind. I refer to the religion of Gaelic football and hurling, especially football. The Vatican of this religion is at Croke Park, Dublin, but there are bishoprics and parishes throughout all Ireland. The climactic ceremony of the year is the All-Ireland Football Final, played in the Dublin Vatican before an ecstatic congregation of almost seventy thousand souls. Gaelic football is a wonderful game, especially in Kerry, although other countries, such as Dublin, Offaly, Cork and Galway, are not so bad either, particularly when Kerry are not around. Seriously, the G.A.A. is a powerful, thriving, influential organization. But again, like the church, it tends to be maddeningly conservative. And it doesn't do enough for the cultural, educational life of young people. It should have a much more positive and comprehensive scholarship and grant system. The G.A.A. should provide more than splendid entertainment; it should broaden the intellectual horizons of its most gifted youngsters. But broadness has never characterized G.A.A. policies. Too often, these policies have been narrow, fixed and self-righteous. If only the G.A.A. bureaucrats thought and acted with the energy, devotion and imagination shown by youngsters playing hurling and football, then it would play a much deeper and more significant part in Irish life. People give a lot of time and attention to the games; but, apart from entertainment and the occasional modest cultural gesture, not much is given back to the people, especially to the young. Ireland has now the youngest population in Europe. In that statistic lies the country's strongest hope for the future. Throughout the countryside, one can see that the young people are becoming more free in themselves. There are many reasons for this increasing freedom, not least of which is that the physical punishment of children is no longer permitted in National Schools. Violence against children at home or in school is, we all agree, an act of barbarism. For decades, many children lived in fear of certain teachers. I refer to those unfortunate men and women who, being bad teachers, expressed their frustration by punishing the children they were supposed to teach. The fear and hatred engendered by this kind of violence can last a lifetime. Today, such barbarism (which, curiously enough, was often approved by parents of the victims) is illegal. Children no longer cringe in fear of the teacher's stick. The removal of that fear has contributed to the increasing independence of the young. Independence brings many gifts with it. One of these gifts is a determination to make life less drab or, to put the matter positively, to make life more colourful, more attractive to the senses. For example, most of the houses built thirty and more years ago in the countryside were dull, unimaginative blocks, grey and sullen in their squat depression. I have heard it said that the Irish are visually illiterate, that they simply do not appreciate colour or know about the energizing role it might play in their daily lives. I accept the truth of this accusation, especially in relation to rural life during the forties, fifties and even sixties. It was at that time a depressing experience to pass through many towns and villages; they seemed, to put it bluntly, dead places inhabited by a few shuffling corpses, the few who couldn't make it to the emigrant ship. Now, in the eighties, despite all the talk of recession and unemployment, the countryside is, in purely architectural terms, a much more colourful place; and it is an increasing pleasure to go through these towns and villages that were once so lifeless and grey. But there is still need for more life, more colour. And there are still grotesque, ugly spectacles that repel the eye. I have in mind especially the increasing number of car graveyards throughout the countryside. People all over Ireland are still largely unconscious of the ugliness and pollution created by litter. Many of them will dump their rubbish, including their used cars, just about anywhere. A beautiful landscape, a lovely winding river, a peaceful green field – any of these places can become an overnight dump. Here is one vital area in which children – and adults – must be educated. Disfiguring the countryside is criminal and is all the more infuriating because it is usually done not with any malevolent intention but with a thoughtless, sluggish good-nature: 'Ah sure I only ditched the oul' car in the oul' field. 'Twas the handiest spot and I didn't think there was a trace o' harm in it.' If we don't know what ugliness is, we cannot recognize what is beautiful; and our lives are the poorer for that. Although many country people are still very conservative in almost every respect there is a growing appreciation of alternative ways of living, of other, different styles of experiencing life, especially among the young. This in itself is an animating force and suggests that the future will not be marked by a dull conformity but by an exciting variety. The scars of history will never completely vanish but the wounds they represent may finally be cured. The Irish have proved that they can survive catastrophe; they are now in the process of showing that they can re-discover in themselves and in their children those civilized qualities, feelings, ideas and convictions that were too long subdued, repressed and distorted. But this will happen only if every individual takes it on himself to think about what it means to try to be free. It is the most difficult and the most necessary task of all. Despite a lot of evidence to the contrary, I believe that the Irish, or a fair number of them, are capable of it.

Unusual combination of colours in a south
Clare village.

Haymaking near Kilrush, Co. Clare.

Tea-time, Cork City.

Pilgrims on Croagh Patrick Mountain, Co. Mayo.

Pilgrims on Croagh Patrick Mountain, Co. Mayo.

Door in Roundwood village, Co. Wicklow.

Derelict shop front, Glenealy, Co. Wicklow.

Dingle Agricultural Show, Co. Kerry.

Throwing dice at the Races, Dingle, Co. Kerry.

Turning the soil, Enniskerry, Co. Wicklow.

Farmyard near Bloodyforeland, North Donegal.

Storm at the seafront, Bray, Co. Wicklow.

The Fun Palace, Bray, Co. Wicklow.

Shopfront, Clifden, Co. Galway.

Castletownbere, West Cork.

On Inishbofin Island, off the Galway coast.

Couple outside their colourful cottage, Mallow, Co. Cork.

Waterpump, Ramelton, Co. Donegal.

Window in Little Bray, Co. Wicklow.

Couple in a bar, Rostrevor, Co. Down.

Private conversation in a bar,
Dundalk, Co. Louth.

FOR SALE -
GERANIUMS - BIZZY
LIZZIES AND OTHER
PLANTS.
ALSO PADRE PIO NOVENA
& RELICTS LEAFLETS
30P EACH

Shop Window, Kilrush, Co. Clare.

Shop interior, Miltown Malbay, Co. Clare.

Farm buildings, Kilrush, Co. Clare.

Dan Foleys Pub, (detail) Annascaul, Co. Kerry.

Itinerants, near Cahir, Co. Tipperary.

Itinerants, Skibbereen, Co. Cork.

12th. July parade, Bangor, Co. Down.

12th. July parade, Bangor, Co. Down.

Mural on the Falls Road, Belfast.

Mural on the Falls Road, Belfast.

Winter in the Mourne Mountains, Co. Down.

Winter in the Mourne Mountains, Co. Down.

LANDSCAPE

THE photographs of the landscape of Ireland in this book are strikingly dramatic, covering scenes and moods from North, South, East and West. The more one looks at these photographs the more one grows to appreciate and become involved in the magical drama of Irish landscape. But it should be said that this landscape, like many of the men and women who move through it, is deeply and unpredictably moody. It is possible, therefore, and in some cases inevitable for one to establish and develop a relationship with landscape: one mood feeds off but also stimulates another. A man can feel like a March morning or a November night; or he can feel like a sluggish river or a troubled sea. The Irish are often said to be a moody people. If their landscape is any guide, the truth of that observation can hardly be disputed. If one does not relate to landscape, landscape might as well not exist. Conversely, any landscape is richer because human eyes gaze at it and human minds pay it attention.

Given this basic notion of relationship, the most incisive writer about Irish landscape is, to my mind, J. M. Synge. His plays and poems and prose show a deep knowledge and love of landscape in all its variety and complexity. And we never lose sight of the fact that the landscape is being observed by a human being whose heart is moved by what he sees. His eyes criticise, embrace, disdain, judge, evaluate. Furthermore, Synge often gives us a graphic description of the extraordinary influence that landscape can have on people, and how it can vary in that influence from soothing consolation to uncontrollable madness. In this particular instance, we get a strong sense of landscape as being almost an avid, predatory creature crouched in hungry anticipation over the lonely, vulnerable lives of men:

> Among the cottages that are scattered through the hills of County Wicklow I have met with many people who show in a singular way the influence of a particular locality. These people live for the most part beside old roads and pathways where hardly one man passes in the day, and look out all the year on unbroken barriers of heath. At every season heavy rains fall for often a week at a time, till the thatch drips with water stained to a dull chestnut and the floor in the cottages seems to be going back to the condition of the bogs near it.

Then the clouds break, and there is a night of terrific storm from the south-west – all the larches that survive in these places are bowed and twisted towards the point where the sun rises in June – when the winds come down through the narrow glens with the congested whirl and roar of a torrent, breaking at times for sudden moments of silence that keep up the tension of the mind. At such times the people crouch all night over a few sods of turf and the dogs howl in the lanes.

When the sun rises there is a morning of almost supernatural radiance, and even the oldest men and women come out into the air with the joy of children who have recovered from a fever. In the evening it is raining again. This peculiar climate, acting on a population that is already lonely and dwindling, has caused or increased a tendency to nervous depression among the people, and every degree of sadness, from that of the man who is merely mournful to that of the man who has spent half his life in the mad-house, is common among these hills. Not long ago in a desolate glen in the south of the country I met two policemen driving an ass-cart with a coffin on it, and a little further on I stopped an old man and asked him what had happened.

'This night three weeks', he said, 'there was a poor fellow below reaping in the glen, and in the evening he had two glasses of whiskey with some other lads. Then some excitement took him, and he threw off his clothes and ran away into the hills. There was great rain that night, and I suppose the poor creature lost his way, and was the whole night perishing in the rain and darkness. In the morning they found his naked foot-marks on some mud half a mile above the road, and again where you go up by a big stone. Then there was nothing known of him till last night, when they found his body on the mountain, and it near eaten by the crows.'

Just recently an Australian friend said to me that he found it hard to express his feelings when experiencing parts of Wicklow. It was difficult for him to reconcile his appreciation of the beauty of the place with the sense of loneliness that it inspired in him. He had not previously experienced this kind of conflicting response. I asked him to read Synge. And in that writer's pages he found expressed the strange emotions he felt in Wicklow, arising from that moment of contact between the natural loneliness of a man's soul and the compelling power of natural beauty.

I remember lying in the heather one clear Sunday morning in the early autumn when the bracken had just turned. All the people of the district were at Mass in a chapel a few miles away, so the valleys were empty, and there was nothing to be heard but the buzzing of a few late bees and the autumn song of thrushes. The sky was covered with white radiant clouds, with soft outlines, broken in a few places by lines of blue sky of wonderful delicacy and clearness. In a little while I heard a step on a path beneath me, and a tramp came wandering round the bottom of the hill. There was a spring below where I was lying, and when he reached it he looked round to see if anyone was watching him. I was hidden by the ferns, so he knelt down beside the water, where there was a pool among the stones, pulled his shirt over his head, and began washing it in the spring. After a little he seemed satisfied, and began wringing the water out of it; then he put it on, dripping as it was, buttoned his old coat over it, and wandered on towards the village, picking blackberries from the hedge.

Before he was quite out of sight the first groups of people on their way home from the chapel began to appear on the paths round the hill, and I could hear the jolting of heavy outside cars. By his act of primitive cleanness this man seemed to have lifted himself also into the mood of the sky, and the indescribably half-plaintive atmosphere of the autumn Sundays of Wicklow. I could not pity him. The cottage men with their humour and simplicity and the grey farm-houses they live in have gained in a real sense – 'Infinite riches in a little room', while the tramp has chosen a life of penury with a world for habitation.

Countless Irish songs, ballads, poems and stories deal with landscape and with local places. There is no hill, valley, lake, glen, headland, bog, mountain or river in Ireland that isn't rich with legend. Even little fields have names; and the names have stories. When Arthur Young toured Ireland between 1776 and 1779, he, as a good Englishman, had his own feelings about the Boyne. Reading this, one realizes once again how saturated in history the Irish landscape is. It is a treasure-house of memories of battles lost and won, of undying loyalties and unpardonable treacheries, of ancient passions that, even now, always smoulder and often burn. This was written over two hundred years ago, but it has a contemporary ring. And notice how immediately and intensely Young relates to the landscape.

To the field of battle on the Boyne. The view of the scene from a rising ground which looks down upon it is exceedingly beautiful, being one of the completest landscapes I have seen. It is a vale, losing itself in front between bold declivities, above which are some thick woods and distant country. Through the vale the river winds and forms an island, the point of which is tufted with trees in the prettiest manner imaginable; on the other side a rich scenery of wood, among which is Dr Norris's house. To the right, on a rising ground on the banks of the river, is the obelisk, backed by a very bold declivity. Pursued the road till near it, quitted my chaise, and walked to the foot of it. It is founded on a rock which rises boldly from the river. It is a noble pillar, and admirably placed. I seated myself on the opposite rock, and indulged the emotions which, with a melancholy not unpleasing, filled my bosom, while I reflected on the consequences that had sprung from the victory here obtained. Liberty was then triumphant. May the virtues of our posterity secure that prize which the bravery of their ancestors won! Peace to the memory of the Prince to whom, whatever might be his failings, we owed that day memorable in the annals of Europe!

Some parts of Ireland are so famous for their beauty that it is hard to write about them without falling into clichés. And clichés are so stale that we tend to transfer our distaste for them on the place or places that inspired them. This should not be so. Killarney, for example, is called Beauty's Home, and not without reason. The town itself is, to say the least, no work of art (I have heard the line of a song 'By Killarney's lakes and dells' parodied as 'By Killarney's lanes and smells'), but the surrounding countryside can, at moments, justify the claim of another song, that Killarney is 'a little bit of heaven'. Long before the clichés gathered around Killarney's name, Arthur Young recorded its beauty. If the word 'magnificence' has completely lost its meaning to you, (and in this age of babble and gabble, many words have lost their meaning), you will re-discover that meaning around Killarney. In certain respects, not much has changed since Arthur Young's eyes opened to that landscape, more than two hundred years ago.

Soon entered the wildest and most romantic country I had anywhere seen; a region of steep rocks and mountains which continued for nine or ten miles, till I came in view of Muckross. There is something magnificently wild in this stupendous scenery, formed to impress the mind with a certain species of terror. All this tract has a rude and savage air, but parts of it are strikingly interesting; the mountains are bare and rocky, and of a great magnitude; the vales are rocky glens, where a mountain stream tumbles along the roughest bed imaginable, and receives many torrents, pouring from clefts, half over-hung with shrubby wood; some of these streams are seen, and the roar of others heard, but hid by vast masses of rock. Immense fragments, torn from the precipices by storms and torrents, are tumbled in the wildest confusion, and seen to hang rather than rest upon projecting precipices. Upon some of these fragments of rock, perfectly detached from the soil, except by the side on which they lie, are beds of black turf, with luxuriant crops of heath, etc., which appeared very curious to me, having nowhere seen the like; and I observed very high in the mountains – much higher than any cultivation is at present, on the right hand – flat and cleared spaces of good grass among the ridges of rock, which had probably been cultivated, and proved that these mountains were not incapable from climate of being applied to useful purposes. From one of these heights I looked forward to the Lake of Killarney at a considerable distance, and backward to the river Kenmare; came in view of a small part of the upper lake, spotted with several islands, and surrounded by the most tremendous mountains that can be imagined, of an aspect savage and dreadful. From this scene of wild magnificence, I broke at once upon all the glories of Killarney.

Writing about the actual land, the clay of Ireland, I said that it is a genuine giver and an insatiate taker; that it will swallow all in the end. And I do not mean merely human workers, those who give their days to the land. I mean also history, myth, sagas, stories, ballads, legends, runes, songs, riddles, secrets, silences. The landscape of Ireland witnesses all and absorbs all. But there is always this connection, this relationship, between people and landscape, no matter how latent, subdued, or apparently lost it may become. I have also mentioned the intensely *dramatic* nature of much Irish landscape. Near the turn of this century, Synge went to the Aran Islands and noticed there the intense relationship between people and nature. In the following passage, he describes the reaction of women to the burial of an old woman. What strikes the reader is the primitively articulate cry of rage against death and the universe that these women are capable of. This relationship is elemental and, as such, eternal, no matter how repressed it may have become in the psyche of contemporary man. Do we bury what is most real in our pursuit of the ephemeral? 'The morning had been beautifully fine,' writes Synge, 'but as they lowered the coffin into the grave, thunder rumbled overhead and hailstones hissed among the bracken.' Then Synge continues:

In Inishmaan one is forced to believe in a sympathy between man and nature, and at this moment, when the thunder sounded a death peal of extraordinary grandeur above the voices of the women, I could see the faces near me stiff and drawn with emotion. When the coffin was in the grave, and the thunder had rolled away across the hills of Clare, the keen broke out again more passionately than before. This grief of the keen is no personal complaint for the death of one woman over eighty years, but seems to contain the whole passionate rage that lurks somewhere in every native of the island. In this cry of pain the inner consciousness of the people seems to lay itself bare for an instant, and to reveal the mood of beings who feel their isolation in the face of a universe that wars on them with winds and seas. They are usually silent, but in the presence of death all outward show of indifference or patience is forgotten, and they shriek with pitiable despair before the horror of the fate to which they all are doomed.

Before they covered the coffin an old man kneeled down by the grave and repeated a simple prayer for the dead.

There was irony in these words of atonement and Catholic belief spoken by voices that were still hoarse with the cries of pagan desperation.

The lives of people tend to be dominated by systems of religion, morality, law, government, economics and politics. Such systems add up to a kind of free cage of civilization. People's lives often change in accordance with changes in the systems under which they live. The life of landscape tends to resist change much more forcefully. In parts of Ireland, from Kerry to Connemara to Donegal to Antrim to Wicklow, the landscape has retained an elemental silence which many find almost unbearable. Some people cannot live without unceasing noise just as others cannot live without endless light. Among its many offerings, the Irish landscape offers silence and darkness and the terrifying opportunity to get lost! There are those who discover this silence and this darkness and who go to some trouble to experience both. In all our lives to-day, noise plays a constant and for some, a necessary part. One thinks of those transfixed folk going glassy-eyed through Dublin, through many Irish towns and villages, with transistors growing out of their ears. Some cannot stretch on a sunny beach without an insane blare for company. We are all aware, therefore, of Ireland of the noises. But there is a silent Ireland too, which seems as old as time itself, and this is an Ireland to enter and wander about in, where one may stumble on oneself, encounter thoughts and feelings apparently dead and buried, touch and enjoy the mystery of that silence which the modern world finds increasingly intolerable, largely, I suspect, because it might lead to some degree of surprising self-knowledge. I have to conclude from this that most noise is helplessly, dangerously, brutishly ignorant and very bad for the soul. So go out, young man, young woman, and seek the revealing silence of Ireland. Discover the landscape that leads you towards yourself.

I have dwelt at some length, as these photographs do, on the dramatic aspect of Irish landscape. But parts of Ireland are not all as dramatic as many of the places I've touched on, and yet they have their own special magic. Some of the Midland and other counties, for instance, are quiet and reticent by comparison with most of that country stretching from Kerry to Donegal, and yet they are deeply attractive in different ways. Anyone who has been through Offaly, for example, will know what I mean. Here is bogland, the gentle, deep, fire-giving centre of Ireland. There's peace here, the peace at the heart of deep-down things. That is part of Offaly's unique appeal, just as the infinite moods of masterly Ben Bulben are part of Sligo's, or the hushed repose of rich fields is part of Meath's. The landscape of Ireland is a miracle of variety and change and, so far at least, it has to a large extent resisted the poison and pollution spawned by 'progressive' man. If we become more conscious of our relationship with that landscape, and allow it to deepen and develop, we will safeguard it from all such pollution and pass on to our children a landscape as varied, thrilling and unmarred as that which we have been privileged to receive and enjoy.

Full moon at dawn, Poulnabrone Dolmen, The Burren, Co. Clare.

Early christian standing stone, at Reask, Dingle, Co. Kerry.

Slea Head and Coumeenoole Strand,
Dingle Peninsula, Co. Kerry.

94

Inishnabro and the Great Blasket Island
from Dunmore Head, Co. Kerry.

Low tide, Ballyconneely Bay, Co. Galway.

Bog Lake, Connemara, Co. Galway.

Muckross Gardens, Killarney, Co. Kerry.

The Burren, Co. Clare.

Maumturk Mountains, Co. Galway.

Dawn in the Maumturk Mountains, Co. Galway.

Giants Causeway, Co. Antrim.

Giants Causeway, Co. Antrim.

Dawn mist in the vale of Glendalough, Co. Wicklow.

Glendalough, Co. Wicklow.

Rock formations, Aranmore Island, Co. Donegal.

Beara Peninsula, Co. Cork.

Winter snow on the Great Sugar Loaf Mountain, Co. Wickl

Croagh Patrick Mountain, Co. Mayo.

Sea mist near Allihies, Beara Peninsula,
Co. Cork.

The Tearaght, one of the Blasket islands, Co. Kerry.

Dawn at Inishtrahull Lighthouse, Malin Head, Co. Donegal.

Straw Island Lighthouse, Inishmore, Aran Islands.